VISITING HOURS

Saif Sidari (he/him) is a transnational Arab writer and researcher from Palestine, currently based in Brighton, England. He is pursuing a PhD at the University of Brighton's School of Humanities and Social Sciences, where he teaches part-time. He holds an MA in Creative and Critical Writing from the University of Sussex. His work explores themes of grief and a-temporality, masculinity and queerness, displacement and belonging. *Visiting Hours* is his debut pamphlet.

© 2025, Saif Sidari. All rights reserved; no part of this book may be reproduced by any means without the publisher's permission.

ISBN: 978-1-916938-80-9

The author has asserted their right to be identified as the author of this Work in accordance with the Copyright, Designs and Patents Act 1988

Cover designed by Aaron Kent

Cover image: © Rob Goebel / Adobe Stock

Edited and Typeset by Aaron Kent

Broken Sleep Books Ltd
PO BOX 102
Llandysul
SA44 9BG

PRAISE for *Visiting Hours*

There is an impassioned strength to the vulnerability, a gentle fire glowing within this work. Saif beautifully combines the sweet minutiae of the mundane—life away from home, self-image, sweet treats baked by a mother—with the bitter rage of injustice, oppression, longing and loneliness. Nostalgic narrative is given a realistic sharpness. With a considered, insightful voice, this collection rings out bright and clear.

— Georgina Langford

Visiting Hours is a beautiful mediation on memory, desire, family and the body. Layered with fragility and tension, this is a collection threaded with simmering verse, reflecting on finding oneself and the pains of lost opportunity. Sidari is an exciting new voice.

— Michael Handrick

One thing I love about this fine debut pamphlet is how so many phrases in specific poems resonate with the universal theme of exile—exile from place, family, queer love, even from our own bodies: 'I remember growing up in the tensions—ridiculous / wickedness.' Throughout this moving pamphlet I get the sense that the desired recipients will never read it, but that hope and release is still achieved from 'the pitiless bounties of a letter that can never arrive' as 'inside my playdough body sits an unblinking witness'—and bearing its witness is what *Visiting Hours* thoroughly deserves.

— Simon Maddrell

CONTENTS

WHERE DID YOU GO?	11
SHELTER-CAT	13
UNCLEAN	14
GROWING PAINS	15
YELLOWJACKET	17
NIGHTSTAND SODA BOTTLE	19
VISITING HOURS	20
I WANDER IN A NOOK	22
THE STRANGER	24
TAKE OFF YOUR CLOTHES	26
POSTCARD FROM THE EDGE I	28
PASSENGER	29
DELICATE	30
PINK PILL	31
I CAN BE A POET AND STILL HOLD GRUDGES.	34
AFTER	36
I WANT TO WRITE ABOUT LOVE	37
POSTCARD FROM THE EDGE II	38
CORSETED TREE-BARK	39
THE BEATEN PATH	40
HOMEWRECKER	42
ABOUT THE PITILESS BOUNTIES OF A LETTER THAT CAN NEVER ARRIVE	44
NOTES & ACKNOWLEDGEMENTS	47

Visiting Hours

Saif Sidari

Broken Sleep Books

One need not be a Chamber – to be Haunted –
One need not be a House –
The Brain has Corridors – surpassing
Material Place –

— Emily Dickinson

WHERE DID YOU GO?

I remember growing up in the tensions—ridiculous
wickedness: the half-lighted man who searches for love
in my waistline, orbiting me like in his eyes is all
I could be. My love
who lays me out beneath lamplights,
a flat apathy values my makeup:
pinches parts of me for the right materials, bummed
to come up with so much. I am still
white-knuckled, hoping this one won't leave
without a word, blotting me like oil from his brow.

I don't enjoy picking on my resentments. All of me traces
out of time, a signature of tires on the trail
darkest at the bend: I grew up
a bruise on an arm and a thigh—boys in my class
took to me poorly, at every knuckle a lesson
righting out my foolish nature. And in their notice
I every morning left
my body behind, pitched it
to the hallway, the playground, or the empty
classroom, where I often hid to eat my lunch.

My father jostles me back. I am visiting
my life again: our family dinner, this time together
as opposed to scattered about my childhood
home—*When did I get here?* My mum sits ahead of me
at the table, watching me like I
still have her milk between my gums,

offering me tea like asking, *where did you go this time?*
This is when my father leaves us—leaves himself.
I take the black tea and
by the time my hand finds the sugar, I'm gone again.

SHELTER-CAT

The neighbour's ancient shelter-cat hobbles
for a drink at dawn—a shaggy muff with one eye
and half a tail. She drinks from the shallow pool
my mother poured in the backyard.

She walks as if through a quagmire, at the edge
to eternal sleep, past a bed of cherry tomatoes
ripe and unclaimed. A hive of hanging red heads
ready to be picked, bathed, cut, and swallowed.

In the yard an antique mirror stonewalls
the shelter-cat, her wise amber eye travels her form:
a garden of histories blending patchwork fur
over scar tissue—survival stories in the jetsam.

You see her thread the space like a dream, a brittle body
without a shadow, a relic swinging in the dawn
between life and a rumour, the lone ghost in my yard,
her head bent over the precipice, witless with thirst.

Breakfast's ready! My mother sighs, hunching deep.
She carries a modest feast on her back, a cloud swelling
in the columns of her spine—a river's cycle to feed
and empty, her smile no longer spreading to the eyes.

She pulls at threads in her nightdress—carved
satin upturns to remind us: what happened to her body.
Every seam given tethers the family to her like a beacon, all
the while: stray in our pool, is a floating grey matt in the blue.

UNCLEAN

I can't keep up with how often I find myself
coming apart: bent out of shape—my heart forgets
how to be a heart sometimes. I think what I'm doing
is breathing, oxidising, waiting for the world
between lumpy cushions and mounds of unclean
clothes—I take flight in dreams, and because I live
many lives with many faces, I can also die just as often.

GROWING PAINS

It isn't difficult, really, to swallow things down
to the trace. I unburden every cup
leftover, gone stale in the wait, mounting keeps
on my tongue—I am an installation here
at the stoned shore, my eyes commune with the wintering
ocean, like globed caskets ready to meet their purpose.

   *

I reach for a light, raise a cooing flame
to a rollup: the throat of my shame is tended
by smoke and tar. Longing barters for tributes to return me
a body before all the hands came
upon me like the even-tide, its dominion creeping high
and expecting: I see the boy I was, crowning

with the waves. His callow head emerges
knocked and seeking. I tell time
counting islands of rot that punctuate his face; I wonder
about his slack jaw, or the stranger inside
his oceanbed mouth, taking on water with abandon
like I am not this body, keeping score

as we go. That today is just another day
I could not learn to love the tide, for all its signs
and visitations—the way it exhumes
my every body, every butchered boy in the eddy
folding back his angel-wing, delivers them
like a gathering of headstones. Seventeen

birthday candles, still so strange—the unease to call out
your own name. I flinch, I turn, at last I see
a man settles behind me. He dawns a face not unlike
my own—yet aged, nebulous, knowing—severed
by obsidian bars. His eyes, like an exposed nerve
catching the scene; *I need to know what he can see.*

*

And just like that, my time had come
and gone. The ocean swung its iron maw—the tide
is out of joint. Here is the saltwater, rushing at my hips
and hands. I find myself too late, as the dead
found theirs. Here is our hummingbird heart-
beating at the altar of an altogether different animal.

We all of us watch, on: the caged man drawl,
waving at me, like painting the time of death.
The body I am, now a history of growing pains
as the tide harrows every stone upon the bay.
And I hear him sing to the sombre moons in my eyes
quivering hymns of be still, or I'm sorry, or die.

YELLOWJACKET

Let us ride our bikes in the gardens behind this disquiet—through the splits in these tall snub-nosed fences. Stay close; consider the scrub of pine and January mildew, flecked broad in the neatest justice, not unlike a dream of nonsense: Yes, that floating cabinet where the giant yellowjacket in a yellow jacket lives has always been in my bedroom.

*

My love perches on the words of a foreigner's language, always arriving late, too late, or never at all. We ride through a choreography of patient black oaks and honeycreepers, and I see the day lift from your face the despairing half-story, for a moment. They don't make air like this anymore—a wonder tonic, dressing our mouths in absentia.

*

I lead you further down, away from every timepiece in the big city—it's what the living do. We rest in the canopy, our eyes grasping at the boughs, how they flourish through the atmosphere, and offer to the starlings their winter flightpath. We fashion our watchtower bed from aerial roots, tapping every impression like maples.

Your body steadies mine—we are stowaways, riding the breeze. I take the holy date from your hand; my fingers graze your uncommon skin: your touch becomes a life raft in the sea of my impossible affections.

*

Yesterday is a story—it may as well be someone else's life. I ask you here to search your heart, to pick through the bones of our history together. You are only ever able to swell inside me. We slur the charming truth like drunks and I am fed, just enough to stay this way. I crucify, I betray; I lie so I might come upon the miracle of keeping you.

*

We step off the trail, as yet unheard. My taut clapper neck strikes the belly of a bell, my heart is everywhere, disappearing beneath the waterlilies. In this version, you turn your back on the sprawling mangroves—you cannot recall what it was like: your life before the fences. In this version, I never felt a cleave in your embrace, or the stones in your pockets.

NIGHTSTAND SODA BOTTLE

I left my soda bottle out on the nightstand
uncapped—its neck exposed without a head.
This isn't uncommon practice, if a bit wasteful.
By now what's left inside is lukewarm and limp,
a dark liquid flattened by too much breathing.

I think about reaching for it, to swallow what is
left, to not quit the bottle. If only I can get a grip
around its body, with a name you've probably heard,
for a taste you've no doubt savoured, out in the sun
or slouched on a bed without sheets like mine.

I watch it for the time, in the feeble shadow
hugging its feet like a boy afraid, without a mother.
The bottle so utterly still and quiet, juts in its display
on a cluttered nightstand, like it has been here a lifetime
with no expiration date—like it doesn't care to know itself.

I imagine it must be hard to be something to someone,
but old news—a corner store pick-me-up, taking up space
playing dead on rented furniture. A temporary occupant
standing to attention for nothing, trying to be a soda bottle
instead of mounting the stars. Note to self: *buy coasters*.

VISITING HOURS

Every so often I will find myself unburdening
an old storage box, for the same old photo album
from my childhood—its jacket still white as
bleached bone, after all this time and every hand
interrogating its guts. I surrender this body

as libation. I kneel here, in a generous pour
the wall brushes up my cheekbone, I dig
my fingertips into corduroy, making myself
real again, like the truth is more than just
a suggestion, dragging through the dust bowl.

Well then, I am a lake stone, cast and staid
in my bottom-dweller twenties. I was born
guilty, worrying my mum, who does love me
fallen in her faith-crock, or else filed neatly
down, by the furrows along her fine

spine. Where was I? Falling

on hard times. The album yields, its pages
lurid and, coming apart—whatever that's worth
as the hours strike at me like antlers. It's just
habit going backward: a birthday, my emerging
heads, grandma cupping her jowls, effacing

hands, my mum lying, angelheaded on dad,
unfed, his knuckles graze her constitution.
I travel these withholding faces for the clues

I might have missed, inside their brimstone
bodies—I visit in-time with my ghost tongue.

I trace the film like working the knife, plunging
deep, I search the moment I became a boy
who needs his mommy, or an owl-eyed fawn
branded by predations. A sorry little whelp to be
drowned out—concealed in a clusterfuck

of metaphors. I can't get off the tilt-a-whirl:
I am that boy again, always disappearing
around the men in his life, or self-abandoning
women—there I go, in the dollhouse wilderness
stepping away from the limits of my body.

A phantom hand turns the page; I relive
my mother, then: *do you remember, you at six,
pantyhose on your buoyant head like sheer auburn
hair, a crown, dancing without a care? You're much
too old for this now, of course!* Definitions end

by the clack of a gavel—cute fast becomes
perversion. My hands press on my pounding
temples. A gesture homeward lifts the fog
off the answer: that, sometimes, the truth is
your family are just a bunch of assholes.

I WANDER IN A NOOK

Before the nook to no-place, I was a bell
without its tongue; today
I meet a chorus of dwarves
chiselling through a mine. Then a wayward hobbit
nestled in a hillside, whiling away an eve
or an eye. I was a bell without

a yoke; now I wander in a nook
with every turn of the page—I imagine
my hands can change matter
how a struck match searches the kindling
for evergreen magic. A game of leaping
over the threshold, out of time, at every plunge

springs beyond the mountain, or the Shire—
a beautiful unseen coming alive in catching fires.

THE STRANGER

I did not long for tombs, or the lost frontiers.
What succour becomes a death march, or the days
unseaming trellises in my garden, yet I am known
by lines on a map, and the absences of my kindred?

Without the poem I am the untethered stranger in the flue
of belied histories. Notice, how I dawn my humiliations
at checkpoints—a theatre of documents and proofs. Then
I find my-self, writing a genealogy for the new world.

The barren father declares us *children of darkness*
in the mortal hours—what could I be in the camp of privations
but bones on display, dealer in my own destruction, ripe fodder
for the insatiable canon of Western dreams of the orient?

As luck would have it, I leapt from the vine and arrived
in the ode, in the mother eye, in the consciousness of the publics.
I was buried there; I am buried here—who could look away
while my remains ascend with smoke to the final sky?

TAKE OFF YOUR CLOTHES
> *My mother died today. Or maybe yesterday, I don't know.*
> — Albert Camus, *The Outsider*

I wake in a stranger's bed to create
with my mother: the dawn
like a swarm of crotchety bees
urging this room alive—unveiling
her form by an open door
rattling her pill bottles. This is old magic,
a warning: I run my fingertips
along the thick of his hairy thigh to learn
I never left. She watches on
like a wound you drown in, time
and again, like losing
your mind: he turns me over
in his hands, a curiosity to be savoured,
his morning eye storied like
jazz, blushing wine-drunk, churning
stomachs: *take off your clothes.*
Here I am, freefalling, upon him
like June rain, a world
in our crowding mouths,
wilderness swelling the plough
by daylight: yet she stalks, stately
as a palace ghost, culling her love
without a word—in the quiet, *will I be*
forgotten? My mother's forgiveness
unfurls the ancestral valley
into which I am
felled, the skies in exile painting
gaunt shadows—I myself, a little more

dead. *Where did you go*
just then? He asks. That we fuck
like braving the tide
into elegies: a wetness decorating my lips,
breakfast, our bare feet lifting
this un-familiar fog
till my body becomes an open field, becomes
dancing, toward the forbidden
domesticities: threadbare, closet space,
coffee brewing
for two.

POSTCARD FROM THE EDGE I

I wear your every absence as a noose
before putting on a show about miracles
of forgetting, how a thing like love happens
to perfect strangers running out of space
they never had, in the way decay strips bodies
or the silences between us; I imagine
how the mouth of a window swallows up
a home.

PASSENGER

In a taxi. Warning signs: the stench
of vodka, *fuck she was hot*, mania
at the lights, too fast, get out,
I'm so horny man, cigarette butts
in a coffee cup, nausea, and summer
heat, busted air con, *loosen up
handsome*, hairy knuckles, hand
off the steering wheel, horns accosting,
motherfuckers, the hard breaks, too fast
at the bend, get out, the meter
rising, *do you like to fuck girls*, laugh
it off, almost home, *let me see
what you've got there*, his hand,
your crotch, a Friday, fare
7.10JDs, travel time 9 to 12
minutes, get out, his breaths
vile, throat constricting, nothing
happened, *you should lose
some weight*, look away, outside
at pedestrians, the sidewalk,
park benches, a family
picnic, my body, going
going,
gone.

DELICATE

This is a hard day to be seen without
my clothes on, when instead I wished to stay
as something imagined. The blushed gentle
tulip, my hands upturned in prayer, I find myself
wanting for replacement: bits of me severed
in her places of mind, where she labours to hold
the wary styles in my gaze, the mash of skin
stretched or spotted—a body poorly arranged,
wear and tear, inflexible as a bad polaroid,
though this she would never say. She asks to see me
waking, to lie in bed with me at the beginning
of each day. She doesn't see why mornings
are hard for me—I dream my life; I live well
even in nightmares.

PINK PILL
The world that we think we see
is only our best guess.
 — Margaret Atwood, *Walking in the Madman's Wood*

I was by a window when I heard
your anatomies move you, in a way
that resembles climbing. A huntsman
arriving—at every step announcing
Creek, creek, thud. And creek creek thud!

You're close. I guess I can't go back
to watching, modest willows, or the season
that strips branches, exposed—nowhere
to hide. I wonder, what are my pink pills
trying to hide? *Creek, creek, thud!*

It was the way your feet struck
uneven, your body is not your body, like you
could be anything. Creeping night
and every door kicked open, shifting
to plant your flag, *and creek creek thud!*

I lay here outstretched—a vacancy
on offer—'room available; breakfast
optional; low prices'. I forget the time
I agreed to accommodate you inside
my body, blunted, at odds with memory.

Creek, creek, thud! I hear your breaths
misfire, crackling fatherwarm, save a door
between us. You have to laugh when
running-for-a-weapon means I prostrate
myself, easy pickings—here is what is left.

I want out. No one ever taught me
how, so I write into the night
my exodus—my mother tongue
strapped like a body on the tracks, outside
of time. Love demands my leaving

your body; the body that disembodies me,
is on me, like a hand-me-down letter
sweater—mine today, stained
with yesterdays: what is bleeding, what is
ejaculate, what is a home-body?

The stink has me drink on occasion
faint moonlight, fresh as a wound,
curtains like gauze bandages hold me
together, before I am emptied—running
out of living-space, cast into perdition

for someone else's honour, whittling outliers
from boys. The innocence that doesn't yet know
the correct way to be, consumed. Pink pills
keeping me from invasions, breaking and
entering, sedate as winter fevers.

I CAN BE A POET AND STILL HOLD GRUDGES.

Here is your meagre frame squaring up against my letter, bouncing vainglorious on the balls of your feet, a costume of peacock plumage, sporting the colours of unbecoming—as if you weren't enough of a cunt already. Flaccid inflections and self-adulation like shrouds upon a miasma; all who know you retching your careless blowhard servings. Your closing argument: *No one can ever hold a candle to me.*

Here is the comedown of seeing, your feckless heart prancing in a hairpin coffin—lodger of the shallows, pumping cowardice to your places of worship, a self-fellating barnacle to be excised. My little love: the oxy-moronic wasteman, of frugal loyalties, mutilated, calculations, *Nothing I do is ever an accident.* For years I wore you close as I do my skin—that's on me, for taking years coming to terms with your wreath of fanciful personalities—none of which will ever make you British. My closing argument.

AFTER

I told myself I would make it, to The Roundhill—a mourning
for mine. Summer birds, descending blazestones around my eyes
watching children dawdle through the procession, billowing clouds
where their mouths used to be. They are our children who wear our bodies
like an invitation to see, our unbidden grief crouching behind doors
of our own making. Listen for the whimpers, crowding halls in spooled
hearts, a wicked boom springing up to the rafters—the home untended
is a desecration, upon itself, gasping, gone, booze-stains cradling the keep…

I forget where I am sometimes. A stiff tongue sits between my jaws, a full set
of gnashing teeth, locked in ceremony. I see, then, how the clocks hurtle, inside
hamster wheels, hours wane in the swelling heat, this wretchedness arriving
without prayer, like something fought for, a debt—we are all us citizens of the clock.
And the tree, leaden with pomegranates, dead languages, and a world becoming
in an instant, what takes from you—from me. I wade against this undertow
adorned by the attentions of my ghosts. Always I feel about them before
I can think about them, propelling my bones, strapping me in, with afters.

I WANT TO WRITE ABOUT LOVE

I wanted to write about love. And I found myself wishing
my mother would stop praying for me—there is no hope for me
inside her prayers. She straps her dream on the neck of an unknown
patron—I am her son but her son never existed. What can love mean
in unseeing eyes? My truest light travels from an extinguished star;
it carries stories of my absences, my distance—it penetrates an alien sky.
What is there to look up to in the big city? Her heart searches for me
and finds unsparing darkness. She carves from it her false child—I
watch her bake, wet and knead the dough, leave it to rise, tear it apart,
righting it to shape, stuffing it with store-bought filling, singeing it good
to be consumed by the family. My mercurial bodies become a landscape
for conquest, a displacement upon a displacement, a letter that will never
arrive again—goodbye Sycamore tree, goodbye good trouble, good-
bye her smile.

POSTCARD FROM THE EDGE II

I think a lot about what I might say—the unsayable
sweetness of a clenched heart, how it rakes my body
through a pyre of submissions, cigarettes, stretched
condoms, my jaw tender when reciting pointless words
that aren't the syllables of your name—a hymn of my
doom: gritting my teeth I soak the mass, in gasoline
and light a match the shape of a man on his knees
begging at an altar by the soles of your feet—Big God
quiet his mind, and the shrieking angels behind his eyes,
so we may finally emerge, softer, fuller, filthier, unmoored
—free!

CORSETED TREE-BARK

I want you   to wet my mouth
with permission   tell it to hunger
your heirloom on my tongue
while I mouth   d e l i c a c y

Creep upon this thirst
in the thick shade   of a hecatomb tree
with moss corseted tree-bark and
pomegranates of good shame

Vindicate me   pumping hearts
are grenade pins   so come
back to me   whole and wanting
justice   shackles are other people

Tell it to the salt in the sand
lapping up the waves   how they broke
my   back   and called it
breathing!

Let your hands sink   deep in my hair
my captain   firm at his helm
Look at me   you instruct
that I might see   you

are drowning me   and I am fed
the truth   spilling into me
reminding me how I was
alive   my first time

THE BEATEN PATH

We felt good, falling through the country, clouding at the arch
of a pale fire—the rudderless poetry I want to love, the first time
then never again. What might it have looked like to love you
from the beginning? And whose beginning, yours
or mine? We act out your every promise, our paper-crane pirouette
through the good life, you and me despite the histories, roach-infested
motels and sinus infections, coco-dusted almonds and you
talking yourself up at dinner parties—the hero who loves to love
fractured things, warping my disappearance
into accolades.

HOMEWRECKER
> *"Does a dream fall sick like the dreamers? ...*
> *Can a people be born on the guillotine?"*
>   — Mahmoud Darwish, We Are Entitled to Love Autumn

I only ever know myself hanging, in the exulted tempest   untouched
by nativities—the possibilities of my name
emptied to the firmaments, which could not care to claim me
yet labour to intubate the clouds, blithely feeding my body to the greying
furies. My own jettisoned   to the moors, a bay of white
polyester sheets, illuminated by ornate keys, bandaged
      after Catastrophe. A world
disappearing   from my grandfather's memory—exit wounds. *I can't find*
      your grandmother.
I cradle his hand, stitching back time, *She died three years ago, seedi*. He recalls
his own key, cloaked in his jubbah, wields it like a prayer, the copper right
of return   remains, welded to his frame, this despite
the bulldozer, rending our home in its maw. Hatchet season, entitled
homewrecker, who kneads our histories into spoils   tragedy-capital to make
      victim of an other,
blood mixing in the mortar. A communion of extolled myths
migrating at the beak of an arrow, toward new beginnings, new ceaseless
wounding, 'cleansing' means   cleaving. The net at my lips gathering
      dreams—generational springs
nurture me, a stone to resist the tank, cast like going back
in Her arms, where in the mourning we will sing, as we always had,
      a song that is ours. A key
longs for turning locks, unspooling the brow, till I am no longer
scattering, everywhere   a ruin meandering through the trees,
      or immigration offices.

ABOUT THE PITILESS BOUNTIES OF A LETTER THAT CAN NEVER ARRIVE

It will be nighttime soon; they promised us rain in these wretched isles. I skulk to the kitchen to make myself a second cup of coffee when I notice I am still a child, and... the stove, the fridge, the cabinets, the bin, all begin to stretch and swell around me like fountains from a popped faucet.

I wonder if I should have tried harder not to smile at the thought of my dad dying. At twenty-seven, I am my father's child interrupted, dragging his body by a firm stitch in my neck. Then there are the prayer rugs, which have always been coarse against my forehead and the bridge of my nose. It was the first place that taught me how a man's hands on my skin can only ever be wickedness.

I mean... my parents lost me, once in Oklahoma when I was five. Maybe I'm being dramatic but sometimes it feels like they haven't found me since.

At dawn, I sail far from every shore to drain my cup in the sea, barring a bead I keep, tucked close like wings. I acquaint myself this way with the missing parts of who I am, as testaments, ungentle offerings—the rattles of a skeleton child reckoning with the rules of the game.

We're all just making things up as we go along, and I guess there is a kind of confession in that. All of me is a plea to tell the quiet parts out loud.

How the God-fearing man ushers me to a sunless boulevard—he asks, "Have you ever gutted a fish with your bare hands?" True enough, in his hands he brings me apart, till my disappearance becomes his holy ablution, the ink in his sermon pages, his righteous duty fulfilled, the thrum against his vocal chords as he recites the call to prayer.

I hear His summons through a minaret and do nothing about it. I never picked myself back up, off the kitchen floor—my life has always been bigger than I could handle.

Inside my playdough body sits an unblinking witness, recording artist, writing about cruel hands, and all the bingeing, filling back up on, mama's food, crying with the lights, off me, pornography, Norman Fucking Rockwell, emptying, in one of those songs about being lonely in a crowded place.

There is something to it, the homeyness of knowing, where you are, how to get around. Maybe it's just the pills I forgot to take, talking nonsense about nonsense. What else can it mean to grow up in a household on fire that no one but you can see?

I remain, there, buried in the brokenness of these impressions.

NOTES & ACKNOWLEDGEMENTS

A few poems in this pamphlet have appeared in journals, though in earlier versions. While I did rework each piece, to varying degrees, I remain grateful to the editors who first published them:

Ian Chung from *Euonia Review*, for 'Growing Pains'.
Justin Karcher from *Ghost City Review*, for 'Shelter-Cat'.
Kathryn Gray and Andrew Neilson from *Bad Lilies*, for 'I want to write about love' and 'Homewrecker'.

The epigraph opening this pamphlet is from a poem by Emily Dickinson, in a collection selected by Ted Hughes.

The epigraph in 'Take Off Your Clothes' is the first line of Albert Camus's *The Outsider*, translated by Sandra Smith.

The epigraph in 'Pink Pill' is from part IV of Margaret Atwood's collection *Dearly*.

The epigraph in 'Homewrecker' is from a poem by Mahmud Darwish, which appears in a collection called *Victims of a Map*, translated by Abdullah al-Udhari.

I would like to thank Simon Maddrell for offering invaluable editorial support in the development of this pamphlet.

I am especially grateful to Broken Sleep Books and Aaron Kent for taking on this pamphlet—my very first! You can't imagine how much this means to me, so thank you.

Finally, to my chosen family, without whom I would not be here. I love you all, in a way that makes trying to decide what order to list your names here much too stressful. You know who you are. Thank you.

LAY OUT YOUR UNREST

www.ingramcontent.com/pod-product-compliance
Lightning Source LLC
LaVergne TN
LVHW092322080426
835508LV00040B/1266